Diwali

By Trudi Strain Trueit

Reading Consultant
Cecilia Minden–Cupp, PhD
Former Director of the Language and Literacy Program
Harvard Graduate School of Education
Cambridge, Massachusetts

Children's Press®
A Division of Scholastic Inc.
New York   Toronto   London   Auckland   Sydney
Mexico City   New Delhi   Hong Kong
Danbury, Connecticut

Designer: Herman Adler
Photo Researcher: Caroline Anderson
The photo on the cover shows a girl lighting diyas in honor of Diwali.

Library of Congress Cataloging-in-Publication Data

Trueit, Trudi Strain.
  Diwali / by Trudi Strain Trueit, author.
    p. cm. — (Rookie read–about holidays)
  ISBN-10: 0-531-12454-1 (lib. bdg.)   0-531-11835-5 (pbk.)
  ISBN-13: 978-0-531-12454-3 (lib. bdg.)   978-0-531-11835-1 (pbk.)
  1. Diwali—Juvenile literature. I. Title. II. Series.
  BL1239.82.D58T78 2006
  294.5'36—dc22   2006005298

CHILDREN'S PRESS, and ROOKIE READ-ABOUT®, and associated
logos are trademarks and/or registered trademarks of Scholastic Library
Publishing. SCHOLASTIC and associated logos are trademarks and/or
registered trademarks of Scholastic Inc.
1 2 3 4 5 6 7 8 9 10 R 16 15 14 13 12 11 10 09 08 07

Candles and oil lamps glow in the darkness as the sun sets. They flicker in windows. They light up rooftops. They even float down rivers.

The lights are in honor
of Diwali (dee-WAHL-ee).
People of the Hindu
(HIN-doo) and Sikh
(SEEK) religions celebrate
the holiday of Diwali.

A boy and his friends dressed for Diwali

Rama and Sita

Different stories explain how Diwali began. One story tells of a good prince named Rama (RAA-mah). He lived with his wife Sita in India. Rama and Sita were forced to leave their kingdom for many years.

Sita was taken by an evil king. Rama looked everywhere until he found her. He fought the evil king and won. Rama and Sita were welcomed home.

Rama fighting the evil king

Lighting diyas in Nepal

People lined the roads with small oil lamps to light the way as Rama and Sita returned. These lamps are called diyas (DEE-yahs).

Diwali means "row of lights." The holiday is known as the Festival of Lights.

Diwali takes place in October or November. It lasts up to five days in India. It is celebrated on just one day in North America. Diwali also marks the beginning of the Hindu New Year.

November 2007

Sunday	Monday	Tuesday	Wednesday	Thursday	Friday	Saturday
				1	2	3
4	5	6	7	8	9	10
11	12	13	14	15	16	17
18	19	20	21	22	23	24
25	26	27	28	29	30	

Celebrating Diwali at the Golden Temple in India

Diwali is an important
holiday in India,
Bangladesh, and Nepal.
It is called Tihar (TIE-hahr)
in Nepal.

Diwali is also celebrated in
Europe, Australia, Africa,
and most other places
Hindus live.

Ways to Celebrate

People clean their homes for Diwali. They decorate with flowers.

They set out many candles and diyas. Some families have thousands of diyas! People in Thailand make diyas from banana leaves to float down rivers.

Selling flowers for Diwali

Rangolis welcome guests.

The girls in the family create artwork at the entrance to their home. They use paint, sand, or colored rice powder to make designs.

The patterns are called rangolis (rang-oh-LEEZ). Rangolis are used to welcome guests and bring good luck in the New Year.

It is the custom to get new clothes and gold jewelry for Diwali. People buy presents for those they love. They mail holiday cards.

A girl wearing new clothing and jewelry in honor of Diwali

A Hindu mandir

Every family has its own Diwali traditions. Many families get up before sunrise. They may pray at an altar in their home.

Some also go to worship at a Hindu temple, or church. The temple is called a mandir (mun-DEER).

Some families take gifts and sweets to relatives for Diwali. Others sit down to a big dinner. After the meal, they open their gifts. They sing and play cards.

A sweet tray for Diwali

Hindu children giving gifts to one another

It is the custom for brothers and sisters to give each other gifts on the last day of Diwali. It is a reminder to look out for one another always. They wish each other happiness and long life.

Fireworks are an important part of Diwali. Most families gather with neighbors to light firecrackers. Some go to see a big fireworks show. Pop! Bang! Happy Diwali!

A fireworks display near the Golden Temple in India

Words You Know

diyas

fireworks

flowers

gifts

mandir

Rama

rangolis

sita

Index

About the Author

Trudi Strain Trueit is a former television news reporter and weather forecaster. She has written more than thirty fiction and nonfiction books for children. Ms. Trueit lives near Seattle, Washington, with her husband Bill.

Photo Credits

Photographs © 2007: Alamy Images: 17, 30 bottom left (David Crossland), 21 (Janie Wiedel/Photolibrary); Art Directors and TRIP Photo Library: 6, 9, 25, 26, 30 bottom right, 31 top right, 31 bottom right (Helene Rogers), 22, 31 top left (Joan Wakelin); Getty Images/AFP: 5 (Indranil Mukherjee), 29, 30 top right (Narinder Nanu), 14 (Munish Sharma), 10, 30 top left (Devendra M. Singh), 3; Omni-Photo Communications/Dinodia: cover, 18, 31 bottom left.